cat food for thought

Warren Dotz
Masud Husain

cat food for thought

Pet Food Label Art, Wit & Wisdom

INSIGHT EDITIONS
San Rafael, California

INSIGHT
EDITIONS

PO Box 3088
San Rafael, CA 94912
www.insighteditions.com

Library of Congress Cataloging-in-Publication Data available.

ISBN: 978-1-60887-357-9

Book concept: Warren Dotz • Masud Husain
Cover and book design: Masud Husain

Visit the authors at: warrendotz.com • masudhusain.com

Find us on Facebook: www.facebook.com/InsightEditions
Follow us on Twitter: @insighteditions

ROOTS of PEACE REPLANTED PAPER

Insight Editions, in association with Roots of Peace, will plant two trees for each tree used in the manufacturing of this book. Roots of Peace is an internationally renowned humanitarian organization dedicated to eradicating land mines worldwide and converting war-torn lands into productive farms and wildlife habitats. Roots of Peace will plant two million fruit and nut trees in Afghanistan and provide farmers there with the skills and support necessary for sustainable land use.

Manufactured in China by Insight Editions

10 9 8 7 6 5 4 3 2 1

PET'S NAME

Cat lovers have always delighted in feeding and caring for their pets. These pages—through their pairing of rare and quirky images and select verse—evoke that joy, and then some.

The period extending from the early 1950s through the late '70s was not only the apex of independently owned pet food companies and supermarkets, it was also a time when the creative flourish of modern aesthetics was incorporated into label design. And so, many of the pet food labels and boxes showcased here are among the best and boldest that commercial advertising has had to offer.

Look closely and you will see that graphic design was increasingly influenced by comic book and television cartoon illustration, children's breakfast cereal branding, and breakthroughs in contemporary typography and printing.

This wonderful commercial artwork, coupled with quotations about the lovable attributes of felines, is truly food for thought.

NEW
Friskies®
KIDNEY FLAVOR
CAT FOOD

3-FLAVOR
3-Flavor Pet Food Company
Toronto, Canada

Cats always seem so very wise,
when staring with their half-closed eyes.
Can they be thinking, "I'll be nice
and maybe she will feed me twice."

BETTE MIDLER

ACTRESS

3-flavor

BEEF · SEAFOOD · CHICKEN

1 kg

COMPLETE AND BALANCED

NO ARTIFICIAL FLAVOR

3 LITTLE KITTENS
Usen Products Company
Woburn, Massachusetts

We have three cats. It's like having children, but there is no tuition involved.

RON REAGAN

WRITER

3 little
kittens®
8 OZ. NET WT.
IMPROVED
Cat Food

3 LITTLE KITTENS
American Crabmeat Company
Boston, Massachusetts

The fishbowl is an Xbox for kittens.

AUTHOR

LITTLE 3 KITTENS
TRADE MARK
REGISTERED
IT'S ALL FISH
CAT FOOD

9-LIVES
French Sardine Company
Terminal Island, California

The cat has nine lives: three for playing, three for straying, three for staying.

AMERICAN PROVERB

9-Lives®

CAT FOOD

with added
VITAMIN E

ALPO
Allen Products Company
Allentown, Pennsylvania

Call my cat?

No, I just run the can opener.

ANON.

ALPO®

CAT FEAST™

TUNA

NET WT. 15 OZ.

BEG-MORE
American Product Sales
Tualatin, Oregon

Cats seem to go on the principle that it never does any harm to ask for what you want.

JOSEPH WOOD KRUTCH

WRITER

BEG-MORE®
ET WT.
½ OZ.
CAT FOOD

BOLO
Simmons Processing Company
Siloam Springs, Arkansas

Never feed your cat anything that clashes with the carpet.

CAT OWNER'S ADAGE

Bolo
BRAND
CAT
FOOD
READY TO SERVE
CHICKEN
FLAVOR
"LIP SMACKIN'"
GOOD . . .
NET WT. 15 OZS.
425g

BOUNTY
Lucky Wholesale Foods
Redding, California

Anyone who has owned many cats in long succession can define his or her life as a series of furry episodes.

ROGER CARAS

FORMER PRESIDENT OF THE ASPCA

BOUNTY
QUALITY

CAT FOOD

NET WT. 15 OZ.

CAP'N KIT
Ross Food Company
Los Angeles, California

There is no more intrepid explorer than a kitten.

CHAMPFLEURY

WRITER

Cap'n Kit
U.S. PAT. OFF.
CAT
FOOD
Cap'n Kit
MADE BY THE MAKERS OF Dr. Ross' DOG AND CAT FOOD

CAPT. KITT
Van Camp Sea Food Company
Long Beach, California

Cat: Companion in beauty, grace, mystery, and adventure.

AUTHOR

K
Capt. KITT
BRAND
TUNA for CATS
IF PRODUCT OR PERFORMANCE DEFECTIVE
Good Housekeeping
GUARANTEES
REPLACEMENT OR REFUND TO CONSUMER
NET CONTENTS 6 ¼ OZ. AVOIR

CAT-COMFORT
Tennessee Absorbent Clay Company
Paris, Tennessee

There are no ordinary cats.

COLETTE

WRITER

CAT-COMFORT
® TRADE MARK
ABSORBENT
LITTER
The Choice of the Litter

CAT LIFE
Cat Life Packing Company
Chicago, Illinois

Time spent with cats is never wasted.

CAT LOVER'S ADAGE

®
CAT LIFE
CAT FOOD
"FOR THE LIFE OF YOUR CAT"

CATNIP
Vo Toys
Bronx, New York

If you don't talk to your kitten about catnip, who will?

ANON.

PREMIUM
catnip
LEAVES
AND BLOSSOMS
NET WT.
¾ OZ.
VO-TOYS
®
MAKES CATS PLAYFUL!

CATS•MEOW
American Products Sales Company
Portland, Oregon

What part of meow don't you understand?

ANON.

CATS·MEOW
THE COMPLETE
CAT FOOD

CATTY
Edivo
IJmuiden, The Netherlands

A cat is there when you call her—if she doesn't have something better to do.

BILL ADLER

WRITER

Edivo
catty
VOOR UW KAT

CLICK
Astor Products
Jacksonville, Florida

There's no need for a piece of sculpture
in a home that has a cat.

WESLEY BATES

ARTIST

CLiCK
Cat
Food
NET WT. 15 OZ.

CORKY
Staff Supermarket Associates
Jericho, New York

Cats come from an alien world that
we may not understand.

AUTHOR

corky®

CAT FOOD

NET WT. 15 OZ. • METRIC WT. 425 GRAMS

DAD'S
Dad's Dog Foods
Meadville, Pennsylvania

My daughter has a cat and I feed it.

DAVID BYRNE

MUSICIAN

"DAD'S"
CHICKEN FLAVOR
CAT FOOD
NET WT. 15¼ OZ.

DAILY
The Great Atlantic & Pacific Tea Company
New York, New York

Anything not nailed down is a cat toy.

CAT OWNER'S ADAGE

DAILY
BRAND
A BALANCED FORMULA MADE WITH WHOLE FISH
CAT FOOD
NET WEIGHT 15 OZ.

DR. BALLARD'S CHAMPION
Dr. Ballard's Animal Foods Limited
Montreal, Canada

Dogs eat. Cats dine.

ENGLISH PROVERB

2¢ OFF
REGULAR PRICE
DR. BALLARD'S
Champion
WHOLE FISH
CAT FOOD

FIDO CHAT
Quaker Oats Company
Marseille, France

The dog may be wonderful prose,
but only the cat is poetry.

FRENCH PROVERB

PÂTÉE
POUR
CHATS

FIDO
chat

FRISKIES
Albers Milling Company
Los Angeles, California

Friskies
CAT FOOD

Cats know how to obtain food without labor, shelter without confinement, and love without penalties.

W. L. GEORGE

WRITER

A
Carnation
PRODUCT
TRADE MARK
Friskies
CAT FOOD

GIGI
Bush Brothers & Company
Clinton, Tennessee

If the claws didn't retract, cats would be like Velcro.

BRUCE FOGLE

VETERINARIAN AND WRITER

"GEE-GEE"
Gigi
FISH
FLAVORED
CAT FOOD
NET WT.
15-1/2 OZ.

GOLDEN TWINS
T. Passarini Company
Newton, Massachusetts

Cats know all the sunny places.

CAT OWNER'S ADAGE

Golden Twins
FISH and LIVER
1½% BARLEY AND 1½% SOYA BEAN GRITS ADDED
CAT FOOD

HAP-EE
Hap-ee Pet Food Company
Westboro, Massachusetts

The best kind of cat toy has a person on one end.

ANON.

EW
HAP-EE
BRAND
ALL FISH
CAT FOOD

HARTZ MOUNTAIN CATNIP
Hartz Mountain Products
New York, New York

Cats, like butterflies, need no excuse.

CAT LOVER'S ADAGE

HARTZ
MOUNTAIN
Trade Mark Reg. U. S. Pat. Off. Made in U. S. A.
No. 506
29¢
N
Net Wt. 1 oz.
Avoir.
Selected Catnip
HARTZ MOUNTAIN PRODUCTS Corp., NEW YORK 3, N. Y.

HUFF AND PUFF
Huff and Puff Pet Foods
Reedville, Virginia

A cat will assume the shape of its container.

FELINE PHYSICS

HUFF and PUFF
BRAND
CAT FOOD
NET WT. 8 OZ.

JACK & JILL
General Foods Corporation
White Plains, New York

Two cats can live as cheaply as one,
and their owner has twice as much fun.

LLOYD ALEXANDER

WRITER

NEW
Jack & Jill
TRADE-MARK
BALANCED DIET FOR GROWTH AND MAINTENANCE
Cat Food

JONNY CAT
Excel-Mineral Company
Goleta, California

I was such an ugly kid—when I played in the sandbox, the cat kept covering me up.

RODNEY DANGERFIELD

COMEDIAN

JONNY CAT®

Premium Cat Litter

Scoop Formula™

Economy Convenience Pack

MOISTURE ACTIVATED
with Green Gard®
ODOR CONTROL

3/8 lb. PAPER BAGS

KAT-NIP
Safeway Stores
Oakland, California

There is no snooze button on a cat who wants breakfast.

AMERICAN PROVERB

kat-nip®

COMPLETE AND BALANCED
FOR GROWTH AND MAINTENANCE*

CAT FOOD

KAT-NIP
Safeway Stores
Oakland, California

When it comes to knowing how to relax,
cats are the original yoga experts.

PATRICIA CURTIS

WRITER

"Kat-Nip"
BRAND
CAT FOOD
NET WT. 15 OZ.

KIT-E-KAT
Chappie Limited
Slough, England

Meow is like aloha;
it can mean anything.

HANK KETCHAM

CARTOONIST

KIT-E-KAT
THE COMPLETE AND NOURISHING
CAT FOOD

KITTY QUEEN
Demco Packing Company
Los Angeles, California

As every cat owner knows, nobody owns a cat.

ELLEN PERRY BERKELEY

WRITER

Kitty Queen
CHOPPED KIDNEY
CAT FOOD

KITTY SPRAY
Pet Accessories Company
New York, New York

I gave my cat a bath the other day. . . . He sat there, he enjoyed it, it was fun for me. The fur would stick to my tongue, but other than that . . .

STEVE MARTIN

COMEDIAN

NET CONTENTS 6 OZ.
98¢
KITTY
COMFORT
SPRAY
Kills FLEAS, LICE, TICKS
STOPS SCRATCHING
DOG COMFORT SAN FRANCISCO, CALIF.

KOZY KITTEN
Mavar Shrimp & Oyster Company
Biloxi, Mississippi

I really am a cat transformed into a woman.

BRIGITTE BARDOT

ACTRESS AND ANIMAL RIGHTS ACTIVIST

Kozy Kitten
®
CAT FOOD
ET WT.
5 OZS.
PREMIUM
QUALITY
BRAND

LICKIN' GOOD
S. E. Mighton Company
Bedford, Ohio

The four cat food groups: dry, canned, natural, yours!

CAT OWNER'S ADAGE

Lickin' GOOD CAT FOOD

LITTLE FRISKIES
Carnation Company
Los Angeles, California

The other cat's food is automatically preferable to its own.

CAT OWNER'S ADAGE

LITTLE
Friskies®
CAT FOOD
RVE
Braised Liver Flavor

LOVIN' SPOONFULS
Ralston Purina Company
St. Louis, Missouri

Cats have a scam going—you buy the food, they eat the food, they go away; that's the deal.

EDDIE IZZARD

COMEDIAN

Purina
Lovin' Spoonfuls
ET WT.
3¼ OZ.
Liver Dish

LUCKY
The Foster Canning Company
Farmingdale, New Jersey

A black cat crossing your path signifies that the animal is going somewhere.

GROUCHO MARX

COMEDIAN

Lucky
NET WEIGHT 15½ OZ.
CAT FOOD

PET PRIDE
The Kroger Company
Cincinnati, Ohio

A cat can purr its way out of anything.

DONNA McCROHAN

WRITER

NEW
FISH FLAVOR
pet
pride
CAT FOOD
THEY'LL
LOVE IT!
NET WT. 15 OZ.

PETUNA
C H B Seafoods
Terminal Island, California

To start your cat collection, simply open a can of tuna.

ANON.

Petuna
BRAND
TUNA & MEAT
BY-PRODUCTS
FOR CATS

PITTY-PAT
Allied Foods
Atlanta, Georgia

A cat will always sit on whatever you're trying to read.

CAT OWNER'S ADAGE

NEW!
Pitty-Pat
for Kitty-Cats
Cat Food
NET WT. 15 OZ.

PLAY BOY
American Stores Company
Philadelphia, Pennsylvania

Of all the toys available, none is better designed than the owner himself. . . . It comes completely assembled, and it makes a sound when you jump on it.

STEPHEN BAKER

WRITER

ACME
Play Boy
®
New
BEEF KIDNEY
BEEF LIVER
CHICKEN PARTS
CAT FOOD

PRIZE
Certified Grocers of California
Los Angeles, California

If purring could be encapsulated,
it'd be the most powerful antidepressant
on the pharmaceutical market.

ALEXIS F. HOPE

WRITER

Prize®
CAT FOOD
NET WT. 15 OZ. 425 GRAMS

PUSS'N BOOTS
Coast Fisheries
Chicago, Illinois

Most cats, when they are out want to be in, and vice versa, and often simultaneously.

LOUIS J. CAMUTI

VETERINARIAN AND WRITER

3 CANS FREE
← SEE SIDE PANEL
NET WEIGHT 15½ OZ.
PUSS'n BOOTS
MEAT flavor
CAT FOOD

PUSSY CAT
Pussy Cat Food Corporation
Brooklyn, New York

When food mysteriously goes,
the chances are pussycat knows.

AUTHOR

Pussy Cat
FOOD
LET YOUR
CAT DECIDE!
NET WT. 15 OZ.

PUTTY TAT
Payne's Pet Food Company
Fort Worth, Texas

A cat is a tiger that is fed by hand.

CAT OWNER'S ADAGE

PUTTYTAT
NET WT.
15 OZ.
GROUND CHICKEN
FOR CATS

RED HEART
John Morell & Company
Chicago, Illinois

A meow massages the heart.

CAT LOVER'S ADAGE

Morrell

RED HEART

®

CAT FOOD

SAINSBURY'S
J. Sainsbury Limited
London, England

I wish I could write as mysterious as a cat.

EDGAR ALLAN POE

WRITER

SAINSBURY'S
allfishcatfood

SAM
Pet Foods Limited
Melton Mowbray, England

Why isn't there mouse-flavored cat food?

ANON.

NEW FOR CATS
SAM
SAM
MEAT CHUNKS
PLUS SEA-FRESH FISH

SASSY
Bonnie Dog Food Company
Sacramento, California

If cats could talk, they wouldn't.

FRENCH PROVERB

A BONNIE® PRODUCT
Sassy®
CAT FOOD
NET WEIGHT 15½ OZS. AVOIR.
PRODUCT OF U.S.A.

SHOW
Purity Stores
Burlingame, California

It is in their eyes that their magic resides.

ARTHUR SYMONS

POET

SHOW
cat
food
NET WT. 15 OZ.

SWITCH
Allied Foods
Atlanta, Georgia

Switch ... to Switch!

Curiosity killed the cat, but for a while I was a suspect.

STEVEN WRIGHT

COMEDIAN

Switch
NUTRITIOUS DIET
CAT FOOD
NET WT. 15 OZ.

TABBY
Usen Products Company
Woburn, Massachusetts

It's really the cats' house—we just pay the mortgage.

CAT OWNER'S ADAGE

15 OZ.
NET WT.

tabby®

MEAT FLAVOR

CAT FOOD

TOP CAT
Buckerfield's Pet Food Division
Vancouver, Canada

If you want the best seat in the house, move the cat.

CAT OWNER'S ADAGE

Buckerfield's*
15 oz 425 g
Top Cat†
CAT FOOD
NOURRITURE POUR CHATS

TUFFY'S
Pine Lakes Feed Company
Perham, Minnesota

Tough times never last, but tough cats do.

COWBOY WISDOM

TUFFY'S®
NEW!
CAT FOOD
NET WT. 15½ OZ.

TUNA 4 CATS
Portland Fish Company
Portland, Oregon

I am, therefore give me tuna.

FELINE PHILOSOPHY

tuna
4
cats®

ED AND LIGHT MEAT TUNA

FOR CATS

WHISKAS
Effem GmbH
Verden, Germany

A kitten is an angel with whiskers.

CAT LOVER'S ADAGE

whiskas®
met KIP en LEVER

Cat Food: A Brief History

Cats only pretend to be domesticated if they think there's a bowl of milk in it for them.

ROBIN WILLIAMS

ACTOR

In the early days of human-feline relations, cats—the great hunters that they are—were expected to fend for themselves when it came to finding food. This wasn't coincidental but rather a calculated relationship. When people started storing grain and other agricultural bounty, domesticated cats were the perfect solution to catching or warding off the pesky animals enticed by the large stores. And felines—the intelligent creatures that they are—perhaps considered how thoughtful it was of humans to lure their favorite meals to them. In this light, one can see that the history of people food is in many ways directly linked to the feline palate.

But the thinking behind feeding one's cat began to change in the Victorian era, when people started bringing felines from the farmhouse into their urban homes. For example, one French writer observed that his cat, when hungry, hunted the pantry's provisions far more than the house's mouse. Another source recommended feeding the cat twice a day with a breakfast of oatmeal and porridge or white bread steeped in warm milk with sugar, and then a heartier dinner of fish. It would seem that feline tastes were adapted and refined along with their surroundings. This remarkable fact was corroborated by extensive interviews conducted in the 1950s with British cat owners, who confirmed fish as the easy first choice of their felines. Meat was a poor second. Cold milk was the favorite drink, though some cats enjoyed a cup of English breakfast tea. One particular persnickety cat fed largely on pancakes. Yummy!

The story of formalized pet food, however, started some fifty years earlier. At the turn of the century, views on pet food changed with the introduction of the first commercially prepared dog foods. Sea biscuits, the centuries-old sailor's fare of vitamin-enriched, nonperishable, hardened dough, were found to be a favorite treat of shipyard pups and strays. This seaman's food was repurposed into the classic, bone-shaped dog biscuit we are so familiar with today. Along with the incredibly successful marketing of dog biscuits came other pet foods—both dry and moist—marketed specifically for cats and kittens.

Though one might argue that some ingredients in moist canned provisions are unsavory to think about, the availability of supermarket-bought pet food meant that cat owners could take the task of feeding their pets out of the animals' paws and into their own. For domesticated cats, this cut down on the poor nutrition and disease that sometimes arose when kittens were left to scavenge on their own.

Mid-twentieth-century military combat produced another change in the pet food world—a shortage of tin. This meant no more canned foods for a while. But technology for food preservation was prescient, and companies began experimenting with producing dry dog food similar to popular crunchy cereals made for humans. The process involved taking a combination of ingredients—meat, grains, and vegetables—grinding and cooking them together, and extruding the mixture through a tube while puffing it with air to create little shapes. Afterward the food was baked and coated with flavors and nutrients. Soon cat food began to emerge on the market following in the footsteps of this modernized dog kibble.

Over the decades that followed, more and more cat foods started hitting grocery and pet store shelves with varieties of liver, beef, chicken, and fish flavors. Cats and their owners were, and continue to be, spoiled by the plurality of choices, which is an especially good thing for cats who are "finicky eaters." By the 1970s there were hundreds of pet foods on the market, each vying for the attention of cat owners looking to treat their felines to something special. In addition to leaving behind a legacy of well-fed kittens, each brand left a unique visual imprint, making for scores of labels just waiting for the right collector of cultural ephemera to pick them up for more than the fishy feasts they advertised. Luckily, someone had the foresight to snag the best and save them for posterity.

Food for thought is no substitute for the real thing.

WALT KELLY

CARTOONIST

Kittens are natural paper shredders.

ANON.

GUARANTEED ANALYSIS:

Minimum Crude Protein	10.50%
Minimum Crude Fat	2.00%
Minimum Crude Fiber	1.50%
Minimum Moisture	74.00%
Minimum Ash	3.50%

Humor Consultant . . . . Neil Berliner
Book Agent . . . . Peter Beren
Book Editor . . . . Dustin Jones

ACKNOWLEDGMENTS:

Robert Booth, Christine and Greg Freeman, Sherry Harris, Jane Husain, Randy Jones, and Dennis Weiss. Inspired by our furry friends Chairman Meow, Willie, Mickey, Duke, Toby Black, Salty, and Christina Kitzy Witz.

Chicken, Soybean Meal, Ground Yellow Corn, Salt, Vitamins, and Water sufficient for processing. Formulated for taste and nutrition.

Disclaimer: Best efforts were made to ensure the accuracy of the attributions of selected quotes. Notification to the publisher of any inaccuracies will result in an amendment in future editions.

PACKED BY:

Warren Dotz
Masud Husain

BRITE-IZE
CAT FOOD
Nutritious-Pleasing Aroma
NET WT.
15 OZ.

Warren Dotz is a collector of pop culture ephemera and author of eleven books on advertising, design, and commercial label art. His commentary has appeared in *Advertising Age*, *Adweek*, and the *New York Times Magazine*. He lives and works in San Francisco and New York City.

Masud Husain is a graphic designer, branding specialist, and avid collector of American advertising ephemera. He designed and co-authored the award-winning books *Meet Mr. Product* and *Ad Boy* with Warren Dotz. He lives and works in Albany, California.